# INVESTING IN AFRICA 101

**Practical Strategies for Wealth Creation and Legacy Building in Africa**

By Emmanuel Bope and Solange Bope

Calgary, Alberta, CANADA

PAN AFRICAN LIFESTYLE INC.

Authors: Emmanuel Bope and Solange Bope

Printed and bound in Canada

First printing August 2025

Published by Pan African Lifestyle Inc.

Alberta, CANADA

978-1-998780-36-5 Paperback

www.panafricanlifestyle.com

*Africa is not poor, Africans are poor.*

– ***Kwame Nkrumah***

# DEDICATION

*First, we give thanks to Yahweh, the source of strength, wisdom, and the breath of life. Without His grace, none of this would be possible.*

*This book is dedicated to all African dreamers on the continent and across the diaspora who dare to see beyond perceived limitations. To those with vision and the boldness to implement that vision through action, strategy, and resilience, we honor you.*

*To the investors, entrepreneurs, innovators, moguls, and legacy builders who recognize the paradigm shift taking place in Africa, for Africans by Africans, we salute you. You are living proof that Africa's renaissance is not a distant hope but a present reality.*

*May this book serve as a testament to every African and diasporic visionary who dreams, dares, and does, turning bold ideas into lasting legacies. This is The African Dream.*

# CONTENTS

# DISCLAIMER

This publication, *Investing in Africa 101* (the "Book"), has been prepared and published by **Pan African Lifestyle** and its authors for **educational and informational purposes only**. The contents herein do not constitute, and should not be construed as, personalized financial advice, investment recommendations, legal advice, accounting advice, or tax guidance.

Readers are advised that **all investment involves risk**, including the potential loss of principal. Market conditions in Africa and globally may change rapidly due to political, regulatory, economic, or social factors, and past performance or historical trends referenced in this Book are **not guarantees of future results**.

The information presented is **general in nature** and is intended to provide background knowledge, context, and frameworks for understanding Africa's investment landscape. It is not tailored to the financial circumstances, goals, or needs of any individual reader.

**Professional Consultation Required**

Readers are strongly encouraged to:

- **Assess their personal financial circumstances**, including income, expenses, assets, debts, and long-term obligations.
- **Determine their individual risk tolerance**, liquidity needs, and investment horizon.
- **Consult qualified professionals** — including licensed financial advisors, accountants, tax specialists, and attorneys — before making any investment or business decision.
- **Conduct independent due diligence** on any specific opportunity, sector, or country referenced in this Book.

**Limitation of Liability**

Neither **Pan African Lifestyle**, the authors, contributors, nor any affiliated parties make any representations or warranties, express or implied, regarding the completeness, accuracy, reliability, or suitability of the information contained in this Book.

By reading and using this Book, you acknowledge and agree that:

- You bear sole responsibility for your investment and financial decisions.

- **Pan African Lifestyle**, its authors, contributors, and affiliates shall not be held liable for any direct, indirect, incidental, consequential, or special damages, losses, or liabilities that may arise from reliance on the information provided herein.

- Use of this Book does not create any advisor-client, fiduciary, or professional relationship between you and **Pan African Lifestyle** or its authors.

**Good Faith Transparency**

This Book was created in good faith with the intent to educate, inform, and empower readers interested in Africa's economic and investment opportunities. While the guidance and insights provided may serve as a foundation for learning, readers must take full responsibility for their own financial, legal, and investment decisions.

# PREFACE

*Investing in Africa 101 was created in direct response to the overwhelming feedback we received from readers of our previous book, Africa 101: The Pan African Lifestyle Guide to Relocating, Investing & Living the African Dream in the Motherland. That first guide served as a foundational resource — offering practical advice, inspiring insights, and essential steps for members of the global Black diaspora seeking to reconnect with Africa, relocate, acquire citizenship, or explore business opportunities.*

*In the months that followed, we were humbled by the countless messages, emails, calls, comments, and social media posts expressing gratitude for Africa 101. Readers shared how it gave them clarity, confidence, and direction on their journey. Yet a consistent theme emerged: while Africa 101 laid the groundwork, there was a strong demand for something more specialized, more in-depth, and more focused on a subject at the very heart of Africa's future —* ***investment.***

*Investing in Africa 101 was written to answer that demand. Where the first book provided the broad strokes of relocation, culture, and lifestyle, this volume zeroes in on the financial dimensions of Africa's renaissance. It is designed as a structured, professional reference for those who want to understand the continent's opportunities, evaluate risks, and develop informed strategies for sustainable wealth-building.*

*This book situates Africa not only as a place of heritage and belonging, but also as a dynamic frontier of global growth. It offers:*

- ***Historical and Contextual Insight:** Lessons from the past that inform today's opportunities.*
- ***Mindset and Philosophy:** The mental frameworks required to invest wisely and responsibly.*
- ***Sectoral Analysis:** A look at the industries and markets driving Africa's economic rise.*
- ***Practical Guidance:** Strategies, regulatory considerations, and steps for building a purposeful portfolio.*
- ***Case Studies and Resources:** Real-world examples and professional references to help readers move from theory to action.*

*We want to be clear: this is not a book of shortcuts or empty promises. Rather, it is a compass — a resource that empowers readers to approach investing in Africa with knowledge, clarity, and integrity. By blending history, culture, economics, and strategy, our aim is to provide a tool that is both practical and inspirational.*

*As with Africa 101, this book is ultimately about more than information. It is about equipping a global Black community to participate meaningfully in Africa's growth story — not as spectators, but as contributors and beneficiaries of its promise.*

*May Investing in Africa 101 inspire you to dream boldly, plan wisely, and act purposefully — and may it guide you toward building not just financial wealth, but a legacy that strengthens Africa and uplifts generations to come.*

Emmanuel Bope and Solange Bope

**Emmanuel and Solange Bope**
Founders of Pan African Lifestyle Inc.

# AFRICA IS THE FUTURE.

*Africa has 54 markets. We're looking at Africa only. In [coming] years, Africa will be home to a third of the global population of youth. By 2050, one out of every five customers on the internet will be in Africa. Africa in the past decade has, out of the top 10 countries with the fastest growing GDP, five of those markets are in Africa. Retail spend in 2018 was about $1.4 trillion. Two-thirds of that was consumer packaged goods. And it's considered one of the fastest growing regions for consumer packaged goods spending in the world. On top of that, when it comes to profitability margins, it's the most profitable region, bar none, to East Asia.*

– ***Mariam Braimah***

# INTRODUCTION

Who would thought that one of Pan African Lifestyle's most-shared videos on social media would spark the creation of *Investing in Africa 101*?

The clip resurfaced years after its first release, flooding timelines with the kind of fascination usually reserved for championship victories or viral celebrity scandals. But this wasn't entertainment — it was a boardroom.

Four investors sat in high-backed chairs, skepticism etched across their faces. Across from them, poised and calm, was Mariam Braimah — Nigerian by heritage, founder and CEO of Komoyo Insights, a research and development firm decoding Africa's vast and complex markets. Her words carried more weight than any rebuttal the investors had prepared.

Komoyo Insights was not just a company; it was a declaration. Braimah and her team were building with Africans, for Africans — partnering with both multinationals and homegrown enterprises to shape Africa's economic future.

In the clip, one investor leaned forward, his tone sharp, eyebrows raised:

"And you think Africa is big enough to get to a hundred million?"

Before she could answer, another interrupted:

"Are you looking at markets outside of Africa?"

The camera caught Mariam's stillness — not hesitation, but certainty. When she finally spoke, her voice was steady, deliberate, and commanding enough to cut through the doubt in the room.

"Africa has fifty-four markets. We're looking at Africa only. In seven years, Africa will be home to a third of the global youth population. By 2050, one out of every five customers on the internet will be in Africa.

In the past decade, five of the ten fastest-growing economies in the world have been African. Retail spending in 2018 reached $1.4 trillion, with two-thirds going to consumer packaged goods. Africa is one of the fastest-growing regions for CPG consumption globally.

And when it comes to profitability margins, Africa is the most profitable region in the world — second only to East Asia."

Silence filled the room. The clip ended, but its impact rippled far beyond that moment. Millions of viewers leaned closer to their screens — not only compelled by her numbers, but by her audacity.

The reactions across our community were immediate and telling. Many asked why she was forced to pitch to investors who neither looked like her nor seemed invested in Africa's people. Some warned, *"Don't tell them everything."* Others challenged us, *"Tell this to our people."*

The message was clear: if Africa is to rise, the global Black community must lead that investment. We — more than anyone else — should be the ones to contribute, to shape, and to benefit from Africa's growth.

As a Tshiluba proverb from the Kasai region of the Democratic Republic of Congo reminds us:

"Let us go home, before we become guests in our own house."

### Why This Book Exists

That moment crystallized what many already knew: Africa is not a future dream — it is a present reality. But the conversation about investment is often dominated by voices outside the continent, while the diaspora and global Black community remain sidelined.

This book was created to change that. *Investing in Africa 101* exists to equip you — the diaspora, the believer, the builder — with both the vision and the tools to engage Africa's markets wisely and responsibly.

### Who This Book Is For

This book speaks to three audiences:

1. **The African Diaspora** — those whose remittances sustain families and communities, and who now want to transform that support into structured investments and legacy.

2. **Global Black Investors** — entrepreneurs, professionals, and visionaries who see Africa not just as a market, but as a mission.

3. **Allies and Builders** — anyone committed to partnering with Africa on equal, respectful terms, who believes prosperity is shared.

## What You Will Gain

In these chapters, you will find:

- A reframing of Africa's story — from scarcity to abundance.
- Region-by-region insights into opportunities across **North, South, East, West, and Central Africa.**
- Practical examples for investors at every level — **micro, medium, and major.**
- Case studies and diaspora spotlights showing what is already possible.
- Frameworks to manage risk, build partnerships, and create legacy.

This is not a book of hype, shortcuts, or empty promises. It is a guide written with clarity and integrity — designed to help you move from aspiration to action.

## How to Use This Book

This book is designed as both a **compass and a playbook.** Each chapter follows a clear structure:

- **Core Insights:** Key principles and context.
- **Regional Spotlights:** Perspectives from North, South, East, West, and Central Africa.
- **Investment Pathways:** Practical examples for micro, medium, and major investors.
- **Diaspora Spotlights:** Real stories of Africans abroad building at home.
- **Frameworks & Takeaways:** Tools and steps you can apply immediately.

You can read cover to cover or move directly to the chapters that align with your goals. If you're just beginning, start with mindset and opportunities. If you're already investing, focus on strategies, risks, and legacy.

Most importantly: use this book. Highlight it, revisit it, discuss it with peers, and apply it to your journey. Let it be more than words on a page — let it be a companion as you step into Africa's future.

# CHAPTER ONE

## HISTORICAL CONTEXT: LESSONS FROM THE PAST

To invest wisely in Africa today, one must first understand the weight of history. Investment has never been neutral. It has always been shaped by trade, culture, and systems of power. Ignoring history risks repeating mistakes. Understanding it provides clarity and a foundation for building strategies that create wealth for Africans and by Africans.

**Africa Before Colonialism: A Center of Innovation**

Before colonial systems disrupted Africa's trajectory, the continent was a vibrant hub of commerce and knowledge. Far from isolated, Africa was deeply connected to global networks.

- The **Mali and Ghana empires** dominated West Africa's trade in gold and salt. At its peak, the Mali Empire controlled half the world's gold supply. Cities like Gao and Timbuktu flourished as centers of commerce and scholarship.

- **Timbuktu University** attracted students from across North Africa and the Middle East. By the

1500s, its libraries housed tens of thousands of manuscripts, rivaling Europe's knowledge centers.

- The **Swahili coast city-states** — Kilwa, Mombasa, Zanzibar — linked Africa with Arabia, India, and China. African ivory, iron, and gold were traded for spices, textiles, and ceramics.

- The **Kingdom of Benin** developed sophisticated urban planning, bronze artistry, and diplomatic relations with European nations before colonization.

- In Central Africa, the **Kingdom of Kongo** maintained structured governance, taxation systems, and trade links across the region.

Africa was not waiting to be "discovered." It was already innovating, trading, and shaping the world economy.

**The Disruption of Colonial Systems**

The 19th and 20th centuries saw African economies forcibly redirected to serve colonial systems. European nations imposed extractive structures, not development models.

- Economies were reshaped around exports of raw materials — cocoa, coffee, copper, diamonds, oil.
- Infrastructure (railways, ports, roads) was built to move resources outward, not to connect African markets internally.
- Local manufacturing and industries were actively suppressed to enforce dependency on imported goods.

The numbers tell the story:

- Africa's share of global trade fell from roughly **6% in 1900 to under 2% by 1960**.
- Even after independence, **80% of Africa's exports were raw commodities**, compared to less than 40% in Asia.

The lesson is clear: when external systems control the terms of trade, value escapes.

**Independence and the Struggle for Economic Sovereignty**

The independence wave of the 1950s–1970s carried immense hope. Leaders such as **Kwame Nkrumah** in

Ghana, **Julius Nyerere** in Tanzania, and **Léopold Senghor** in Senegal envisioned economies rooted in self-determination and Pan-African unity.

But the obstacles were steep:

- Economies were locked into mono-crop or mono-resource dependence.
- Infrastructure remained geared toward export, not internal integration.
- Former colonial nations maintained influence through trade and financial institutions.

The 1980s and 1990s brought **Structural Adjustment Programs (SAPs)** from the IMF and World Bank. These required austerity, privatization, and liberalization. While they stabilized some economies, they also weakened state institutions, collapsed local industries, and increased inequality.

**Case Study: Cocoa in Ghana**

Ghana and Côte d'Ivoire together produce over **60% of the world's cocoa**. Yet the two nations capture less than **6% of the global chocolate industry's $130+ billion value**. Most profit accrues to European and North

American companies that dominate processing, branding, and distribution.

This is Africa's central economic challenge: not lack of resources, but lack of value capture. For modern investors, the opportunity is to invest in processing, packaging, and branding within Africa.

**Regional Spotlight: Africa's Diverse Historical Foundations**

Africa's history is not a single story. Each region developed its own economic systems, cultural innovations, and global connections long before and during colonial disruptions.

**North Africa**

- Ancient Egypt, Carthage, and Islamic scholarship shaped global history.
- Strong Mediterranean ties influenced infrastructure and trade.
- Today, Morocco and Egypt anchor regional manufacturing and logistics.

**West Africa**

- Gold, salt, and trans-Saharan trade powered empires.
- Colonial systems enforced cocoa, peanuts, and palm oil dependence.
- Today, fintech and creative industries drive growth.

**East Africa**

- Swahili trade cities linked Africa with Asia.
- Ethiopia's independence shaped regional resilience.
- Modern economies are driven by agribusiness, tech hubs, and renewable energy.

**Central Africa**

- Kongo kingdom developed early governance and trade.
- Colonial extraction of rubber, copper, and cobalt left deep scars.

- Today, mineral wealth (especially cobalt in DRC) dominates but governance challenges persist.

**Southern Africa**

- Great Zimbabwe symbolized wealth and urban sophistication.
- South Africa's mineral wealth built global links but apartheid distorted development.
- Today, advanced markets exist alongside high inequality and energy struggles.

**Investment Pathways: Micro, Medium, and Major**

Understanding history also helps frame modern investment levels. Wealth in Africa has always been layered — from family trade to empire-building. The same applies today.

**Micro-Investment (under $10,000–$25,000)**

- West Africa: Support a cocoa cooperative in Ghana with small equipment loans.
- East Africa: Fund a Kenyan agritech startup through crowdfunding.

- Southern Africa: Launch a small retail franchise in Johannesburg.

**Medium Investment ($25,000–$500,000)**

- North Africa: Invest in a boutique eco-lodge in Morocco or Tunisia.
- Central Africa: Develop a logistics company connecting Cameroon and Gabon.
- West Africa: Finance a Nollywood film or streaming platform.

**Major Investment ($500,000+)**

- East Africa: Back a renewable energy project in Ethiopia.
- Southern Africa: Co-finance an industrial real estate hub in Johannesburg.
- Central Africa: Support cobalt-processing facilities in DRC.

**Investor Insights**

- Africa has always been a center of wealth and innovation.

- Colonial systems disrupted value creation, forcing economies into extraction.
- Independence brought hope but structural challenges remain.
- Regional diversity matters — each region offers unique strengths.
- Diaspora and local investors at all levels can engage meaningfully.

**Framework: Investing with Historical Awareness**

1. **Learn the Context**: Study colonial legacies, independence struggles, and structural cycles.
2. **Identify Value Chains**: Look beyond raw exports; focus on where wealth is captured.
3. **Engage Diaspora Networks**: Connect global resources with local opportunity.
4. **Prioritize Resilience**: Diversify investments across sectors and regions.
5. **Commit Long-Term**: Generational wealth requires patience and vision.

### Takeaway for Action

History is not a weight holding Africa back. It is a map, showing what went wrong and what must now be done differently. Investors who understand this history will see Africa not as a passive frontier, but as an active partner in shaping global wealth and legacy.

# CHAPTER TWO

## MINDSET MATTERS: RECLAIMING MENTAL SOVEREIGNTY

Investing in Africa is not only about capital. It begins with mindset. The way investors think — about risk, opportunity, time, and purpose — often determines success or failure before money is even committed.

Africa is not a continent to be approached with charity or savior complexes, nor with reckless speculation. The mindset required is one of respect, patience, and clarity.

**The Scarcity vs. Abundance Lens**

Too often, Africa has been viewed through a scarcity lens — defined by what it lacks: infrastructure, capital, and institutions. This mindset fuels extractive investment models, where outsiders exploit gaps without building resilience.

The abundance lens, by contrast, focuses on what Africa has:

- The world's youngest population.
- Untapped natural resources.

- Expanding urban centers and consumer markets.
- Cultural exports influencing the globe.

The abundance lens does not ignore challenges, but it sees them as opportunities to build solutions.

**Short-Term Speculator vs. Long-Term Builder**

Another mindset distinction is between speculators and builders:

- **Speculators** chase fast money, pulling out when volatility arises.
- **Builders** invest in ecosystems, relationships, and long-term value.

Speculators often leave disappointment in their wake. Builders create legacies.

**The Role of Patience**

African investments often take longer to mature than in developed markets. Infrastructure gaps, regulatory processes, and cultural negotiations can extend timelines. Patience is not a weakness — it is a competitive advantage. Investors who build with a 10–

20 year horizon will often outperform those seeking quick exits.

**Regional Spotlight: Mindset Across Africa**

Different regions of Africa shape investor mindsets differently. Appreciating these nuances helps align expectations.

**North Africa**

- More established infrastructure and financial systems.
- Investors need a mindset attuned to global integration — North Africa connects to Europe and the Middle East.
- Opportunities in logistics, tourism, and renewable energy reward patience.

**West Africa**

- Known for dynamism and volatility. Currencies, politics, and fast-growing industries (like fintech and entertainment) require adaptability.
- The mindset needed is one of resilience and speed — willing to pivot quickly while staying committed long-term.

**East Africa**

- Innovative and entrepreneurial, especially in Kenya and Rwanda.
- Mindset here must be collaborative, engaging with local startups and regional integration (EAC).
- Patience pays in agribusiness and renewable energy, but agility is key in tech.

**Central Africa**

- Resource-rich but governance-challenged.
- Mindset must combine caution with boldness. Transparency and strong partnerships are essential.
- Long-term investors can unlock immense value in infrastructure, mining, and energy.

**Southern Africa**

- More mature economies (South Africa, Botswana, Namibia), but inequality and energy challenges persist.

- Mindset here is about balancing stability with innovation — leveraging advanced markets while supporting inclusive growth.

**Investment Pathways: Mindset in Action**

Different levels of investors can embody the right mindset through practical steps.

**Micro-Investment (under $10,000–$25,000)**

- West Africa: Fund a mobile money agent network in Nigeria.
- East Africa: Join a diaspora crowdfunding platform for agritech startups.
- Southern Africa: Co-own a small retail or service franchise in South Africa.

**Medium Investment ($25,000–$500,000)**

- North Africa: Partner on a boutique hotel or eco-tourism project in Morocco.
- East Africa: Develop a dairy processing facility in Kenya.
- Central Africa: Launch a regional transport or logistics company in Cameroon.

### Major Investment ($500,000+)

- Southern Africa: Back large-scale renewable energy projects in South Africa.
- Central Africa: Finance infrastructure linked to cobalt mining in DRC.
- West Africa: Invest in a fintech company expanding across the region.

These examples show that the right mindset is not about scale of capital, but about approach. Micro investors can think long-term just as much as institutional investors.

### Diaspora Spotlight: The Builder's Mindset

A Ghanaian-American nurse began with small real estate purchases in Accra. Instead of flipping quickly, she reinvested profits into schools and rental units. Over a decade, her portfolio grew steadily, creating income for her family and jobs for locals. Her success came not from vast capital, but from patience, respect, and a builder's mindset.

**Investor Insights**

- Mindset matters more than money in the beginning.
- The abundance lens reveals opportunities hidden by stereotypes.
- Builders outperform speculators in Africa's long-term story.
- Patience is not passive — it is strategic.
- Mindset must adapt regionally across Africa.

**Framework: Cultivating the Investor Mindset**

1. **Check Your Lens:** Scarcity or abundance? Extractive or generative?
2. **Define Your Role:** Speculator or builder?
3. **Set Timelines:** Think in decades, not months.
4. **Adapt to Region:** Recognize North, South, East, West, and Central differences.
5. **Align with Purpose:** Profit matters, but so does legacy.

### Takeaway for Action

Africa rewards those who think long-term, respect context, and embrace abundance. The right mindset is not about ignoring risks but about seeing through them to possibilities. For the diaspora and allies, this is more than investment — it is vision, patience, and legacy in action.

# CHAPTER THREE

## THE PARADIGM SHIFT AND THE OPPORTUNITY WINDOW

Africa is often spoken of as "the future," but opportunities are already here. The continent's fast-growing cities, youthful demographics, natural wealth, and cultural influence are creating new markets every year. For investors — whether diaspora professionals, small entrepreneurs, or institutions — the challenge is not whether opportunities exist, but how to identify, enter, and scale them.

**Growth Sectors Defining Africa's Future**

1. **Agribusiness**
    - Africa holds **60% of the world's uncultivated arable land.**
    - By 2030, the African food market is projected to reach **$1 trillion.**
    - Opportunities span farming, processing, logistics, and exports.
2. **Renewable Energy**
    - Over **600 million Africans lack access to electricity.**

   - Solar, wind, and hydropower projects are growing rapidly, attracting diaspora and global capital.
   - Mini-grids and off-grid solutions are especially transformative.

3. **Technology & Innovation**
   - Africa has over **600 million mobile phone users.**
   - Fintech is booming (mobile money transactions exceed $800 billion annually).
   - Tech hubs from Lagos to Nairobi attract global venture capital.

4. **Real Estate & Infrastructure**
   - Africa's cities are expanding — Lagos, Kinshasa, and Cairo will rank among the world's largest by 2050.
   - Housing, commercial spaces, and logistics infrastructure are critical needs.

5. **Cultural Industries**
   - Nollywood produces more films than Hollywood.
   - Afrobeats and African fashion are global exports.
   - Creative industries generate jobs while shaping global culture.

6. **Healthcare & Education**
    - Africa's healthcare system faces major gaps, creating opportunities in clinics, telemedicine, and pharmaceuticals.
    - Education technology and private schools are growing as parents demand quality learning.

**Regional Spotlight: Opportunities by Region**

**North Africa**

- Manufacturing, renewable energy (Morocco is a solar leader), and logistics tied to Europe and the Middle East.
- Tourism remains vital, with Egypt and Tunisia drawing millions annually.

**West Africa**

- Nigeria and Ghana lead in fintech, entertainment, and real estate.
- Côte d'Ivoire and Senegal show growth in agribusiness and infrastructure.
- Energy resources continue to dominate, but diversification is rising.

**East Africa**

- Kenya is a fintech and tech hub.

- Ethiopia and Tanzania drive agribusiness and manufacturing.
- Renewable energy, especially hydropower and geothermal, is expanding.

**Central Africa**

- DRC dominates mining, producing over 70% of the world's cobalt.
- Cameroon and Gabon show opportunities in timber, agriculture, and energy.
- Infrastructure gaps remain wide, but logistics and services are growth points.

**Southern Africa**

- South Africa anchors finance, retail, and industrial capacity.
- Zambia and Botswana have mining and agribusiness opportunities.
- Renewable energy and logistics are growth sectors as the region diversifies.

**Investment Pathways: Micro, Medium, Major**

**Micro-Investment (under $10,000–$25,000)**

- West Africa: Support a small cocoa-processing cooperative in Ghana.
- East Africa: Back a Kenyan mobile money agency or agritech startup via crowdfunding.

- Southern Africa: Invest in a small food retail outlet in Johannesburg or Lusaka.

**Medium Investment ($25,000–$500,000)**

- North Africa: Launch a mid-size eco-tourism venture in Morocco or Tunisia.
- East Africa: Develop a dairy or coffee-processing plant in Tanzania.
- West Africa: Partner in a Nollywood production company or digital distribution platform.

**Major Investment ($500,000+)**

- Central Africa: Finance large-scale cobalt or copper value-add facilities in DRC.
- East Africa: Build renewable energy projects (solar or geothermal plants).
- Southern Africa: Invest in industrial real estate or logistics hubs in South Africa.

**Diaspora Spotlight: Opportunity Meets Purpose**

- **Tech & Diaspora:** A Nigerian-American software engineer co-founded a Lagos-based fintech that raised millions in global venture capital while transforming digital payments locally.
- **Healthcare:** A Ghanaian-British doctor launched a private hospital in Accra, reinvesting diaspora income into healthcare infrastructure.

- **Agriculture:** A Kenyan-Canadian entrepreneur partnered with local farmers to launch an organic produce export business.

Each began with different levels of capital, but all shared a long-term vision and partnership approach.

**Investor Insights**

- Africa's opportunities are diverse, spanning agribusiness, energy, tech, real estate, and culture.
- Regional strengths differ, requiring context-specific strategies.
- Micro investors can start small but meaningful; medium investors scale businesses; major investors shape industries.
- Diaspora involvement proves that purpose-driven investment can be profitable and impactful.

**Framework: Identifying Opportunity**

1. **Choose Your Sector:** Align with your expertise or passion.
2. **Understand Regional Fit:** Match sector strengths with regional potential.
3. **Define Your Level:** Micro, medium, or major investment.
4. **Engage Partners:** Local entrepreneurs and diaspora networks are key.
5. **Plan Long-Term:** Build for growth, not quick exit.

### Takeaway for Action

Africa's opportunity is real and immediate. Whether through a $5,000 startup partnership or a multimillion-dollar energy project, investors can enter at their own scale. The key is aligning opportunity with mindset, region, and purpose. This is not charity. It is the work of building Africa's future — and every level of investor can take part.

# CHAPTER FOUR

## THE AFRICAN OPPORTUNITY: A CONTINENT ON THE RISE

No market is without risk. The difference with Africa is that risks are often exaggerated while rewards are underestimated. For investors — whether small or large — the goal is not to avoid risk entirely, but to manage it wisely while positioning for outsized returns.

**The Nature of Risk in Africa**

1. **Currency Volatility**
    - Many African currencies fluctuate sharply against the dollar and euro.
    - Inflation can also impact purchasing power.
2. **Political & Regulatory Uncertainty**
    - Elections, policy shifts, and governance issues can affect businesses.
    - Corruption and bureaucracy remain challenges in certain markets.
3. **Infrastructure Gaps**
    - Transport, energy, and logistics are underdeveloped in parts of Africa.
    - This can slow projects, but also creates opportunities for solutions.

4. **Social and Cultural Dynamics**
    - Misaligned community engagement can derail projects.
    - Understanding local culture and building trust are essential.

**The Scale of Reward**

Despite risks, Africa consistently delivers higher growth potential than many mature markets:

- Six of the world's **ten fastest-growing economies** are in Africa.
- Returns on investment in Africa can be **two to three times higher** than global averages in sectors like telecom, fintech, and agribusiness.
- The long-term demographic dividend — Africa's young population — is unmatched anywhere in the world.

The central principle is this: **high risk, high reward — but mitigatable with strategy.**

**Regional Spotlight: Risk and Reward by Region**

**North Africa**

- Risks: Political transitions (e.g., Tunisia, Egypt) and dependence on European markets.
- Rewards: Strong infrastructure, renewable energy, and tourism opportunities.

**West Africa**

- Risks: Currency volatility (especially CFA franc debates) and political instability in some nations.
- Rewards: Fintech, culture, and natural resources make West Africa dynamic and globally connected.

**East Africa**

- Risks: Regulatory complexity and infrastructure deficits.
- Rewards: Tech hubs (Nairobi, Addis), agribusiness, and renewable energy promise strong growth.

**Central Africa**

- Risks: Governance issues, resource dependency, and conflict.
- Rewards: Immense mineral wealth and untapped energy potential.

**Southern Africa**

- Risks: Inequality, energy crises, and political shifts.
- Rewards: Advanced financial systems, retail markets, and logistics capacity.

**Investment Pathways: Risk at Every Level**

**Micro-Investment (under $10,000–$25,000)**

- West Africa: Back a fintech startup via diaspora crowdfunding — high return potential, but volatility risk.
- East Africa: Partner with a local farm-to-market cooperative — risk of climate impact, but strong demand for food.
- Southern Africa: Launch a small transport business — operational risks, but high urban demand.

**Medium Investment ($25,000–$500,000)**

- North Africa: Eco-tourism in Morocco — political risk, but stable long-term demand.
- Central Africa: Regional logistics startup in Cameroon — governance challenges, but unmet market needs.
- East Africa: Mid-size renewable energy project in Tanzania — regulatory hurdles, but strong growth demand.

**Major Investment ($500,000+)**

- Central Africa: Mining or energy processing in DRC — governance and infrastructure risks, but world-leading mineral potential.
- Southern Africa: Industrial real estate in Johannesburg — economic cycles, but high regional hub status.
- West Africa: Fintech platforms expanding regionally — competitive risk, but exponential scaling opportunity.

**Diaspora Spotlight: Turning Risk into Reward**

A Nigerian-American investor began with small fintech angel investments in Lagos. Early ventures failed due to poor regulation and infrastructure. But instead of retreating, he reinvested in startups with stronger compliance systems. One of them, later acquired by a global tech firm, generated a return that far outweighed the initial losses. His story shows how resilience and persistence turn risk into generational reward.

**Investor Insights**

- Risk in Africa is real, but often exaggerated.
- Reward potential is high — especially for those willing to commit long-term.
- Risks vary regionally, requiring context-specific strategies.
- Every investment tier — micro, medium, major — comes with risk, but also scalable opportunities.
- Diaspora investors succeed when they pair persistence with adaptability.

**Framework: Managing Risk for Reward**

1. **Identify Real vs. Perceived Risk** — Don't let stereotypes dictate investment decisions.
2. **Diversify** — By sector, by country, by scale.
3. **Engage Local Partners** — They understand context better than outsiders.

4. **Use Tools** — Political risk insurance, hedging, and legal expertise.
5. **Think Long-Term** — Rewards compound when risks are managed with patience.

**Takeaway for Action**

Risk is part of Africa's story, but so is resilience. Investors who prepare, diversify, and partner wisely discover that risk is not a barrier but an entry point to higher reward. Africa's future belongs to those who see both sides of the coin — and are bold enough to act.

# CHAPTER FIVE

## KEY SECTORS FOR INVESTMENT: WHERE THE GROWTH LIES

In Africa, success is rarely achieved alone. Partnerships are not just helpful; they are essential. Markets are complex, regulations differ across borders, and cultural contexts require local knowledge. For investors — whether micro or institutional — partnerships multiply strength, reduce risk, and expand opportunity.

**Why Partnerships Matter**

1. **Local Knowledge**
    - Markets operate differently in each region. Local partners bring insights no outsider can replicate.
2. **Shared Risk**
    - Pooling capital and expertise reduces exposure. A joint venture is less vulnerable than a solo investor.
3. **Trust and Legitimacy**
    - Communities support businesses that engage with local stakeholders. Partnerships demonstrate respect and inclusion.
4. **Scaling Potential**

- Partnerships with diaspora networks, governments, or multinationals open doors to regional and global markets.

**Types of Partnerships**

- **Local Entrepreneurs** — grassroots innovators solving daily challenges.
- **Diaspora Networks** — individuals and groups abroad with capital and global perspective.
- **Institutions** — development banks, chambers of commerce, trade groups.
- **Governments** — essential for navigating regulations and scaling projects.

**Regional Spotlight: Partnerships Across Africa**

**North Africa**

- Partnerships often bridge Africa with Europe and the Middle East.
- Example: Renewable energy projects in Morocco attract joint ventures with European utilities.

**West Africa**

- Informal networks are powerful. Partnerships with community cooperatives in agriculture or entertainment amplify scale.
- Example: Nollywood's global success rests on collaborations between local producers and diaspora distributors.

**East Africa**

- Known for entrepreneurial ecosystems (Nairobi, Addis Ababa).
- Example: Safaricom's M-Pesa thrived through partnerships with telecoms, banks, and regulators.

**Central Africa**

- Partnerships are critical for navigating governance complexity.
- Example: Mining ventures in DRC often require joint ventures with government and local firms.

**Southern Africa**

- Mature financial systems encourage formal partnerships.
- Example: South African retail giants expand regionally through joint ventures with local businesses.

**Investment Pathways: Partnerships by Scale**

**Micro-Investment (under $10,000–$25,000)**

- West Africa: Partner with a local shea butter cooperative in Ghana.
- East Africa: Join a diaspora crowdfunding circle supporting small startups in Nairobi.
- Southern Africa: Co-own a township retail shop with a trusted local partner.

**Medium Investment ($25,000–$500,000)**

- North Africa: Partner on a boutique eco-tourism lodge in Morocco.
- East Africa: Launch a mid-sized agro-processing plant in Tanzania with local farmers.
- Central Africa: Build a regional logistics business in Cameroon with local entrepreneurs.

**Major Investment ($500,000+)**

- Central Africa: Co-finance cobalt or copper processing plants in DRC with government and multinationals.
- Southern Africa: Joint venture in industrial real estate with South African developers.
- West Africa: Strategic partnership with fintech platforms expanding regionally.

**Diaspora Spotlight: Partnership in Action**

A Kenyan-American investor sought to develop renewable energy solutions. Instead of working independently, she partnered with Kenyan engineers, community leaders, and a U.S. diaspora network. Together, they launched a solar mini-grid project serving thousands. The venture succeeded not because of capital alone, but because of partnership — aligning global capital with local expertise.

**Investor Insights**

- Partnerships multiply capacity and reduce risk.

- Regional contexts shape partnership strategies.
- Micro, medium, and major investors all benefit from collaboration.
- Diaspora networks are bridge-builders, not just funders.
- True partnerships are based on trust, transparency, and shared vision.

**Framework: Building Effective Partnerships**

1. **Define Goals Clearly** — What do you bring, and what do you seek?
2. **Choose the Right Partner** — Align on values, not just profits.
3. **Balance Risk and Reward** — Share responsibility fairly.
4. **Formalize Agreements** — Contracts protect all parties.
5. **Engage Communities** — No partnership succeeds without community support.

**Takeaway for Action**

Partnership is not optional in Africa — it is the foundation of success. Investors who partner wisely, whether with cooperatives, diaspora networks, or institutions, will build enterprises that last. Partnerships transform investment from transactions into legacies.

# CHAPTER SIX

## INVESTMENT AND STRATEGIES: BUILDING A PORTFOLIO

Africa's opportunities are vast, but without structure, investors risk being scattered and overwhelmed. Strategy transforms ambition into results. This chapter introduces practical frameworks, region-specific approaches, and clear investment pathways for all levels of capital.

### The Investment Readiness Framework

Before committing capital, investors must assess both themselves and the opportunity.

1. **Mindset Check:** Are you approaching with respect, patience, and clarity?
2. **Capital Assessment:** What resources (financial, human, network) do you bring?
3. **Risk Analysis:** Separate real risks (currency, regulation) from perceived risks (stereotypes).
4. **Sector Fit:** Focus on areas where you have expertise or interest.
5. **Partnership Strategy:** Who are your local allies, diaspora networks, or institutional partners?

This readiness check ensures investments are deliberate, not impulsive.

### The Three Horizons Model

African investments require patience. The **Three Horizons Model** sets realistic expectations:

- **Horizon 1 (0–3 years):** Quick-turnaround ventures (retail, small tech startups).
- **Horizon 2 (3–7 years):** Growth sectors like agribusiness and renewable energy.
- **Horizon 3 (7+ years):** Legacy projects — healthcare, industrial capacity, education.

A balanced portfolio spans all three horizons.

**Regional Spotlight: Strategies by Region**

**North Africa**

- Focus: Leverage geographic proximity to Europe and the Middle East.
- Strategy: Export manufacturing, renewable energy, and logistics partnerships.

**West Africa**

- Focus: Dynamic but volatile markets.
- Strategy: Diversify and scale quickly in fintech, entertainment, and agribusiness.

**East Africa**

- Focus: Innovation ecosystems.
- Strategy: Combine diaspora capital with local startups, particularly in agritech and fintech.

**Central Africa**

- Focus: Resource wealth with governance challenges.
- Strategy: Build transparency and community buy-in into every venture.

**Southern Africa**

- Focus: Mature economies with regional influence.
- Strategy: Blend innovation with stability — industrial hubs, retail, and renewable energy.

**Investment Pathways: Strategy at Every Scale**

**Micro-Investment (under $10,000–$25,000)**

- West Africa: Support a small-scale cocoa processing or trading cooperative.
- East Africa: Crowdfund a Kenyan agritech app or solar micro-grid.
- Southern Africa: Invest in township retail outlets or food franchises.

**Medium Investment ($25,000–$500,000)**

- North Africa: Launch a boutique eco-lodge in Morocco or Tunisia.
- East Africa: Build a dairy or coffee processing facility in Tanzania.
- Central Africa: Start a logistics company in Cameroon or Gabon.

### Major Investment ($500,000+)

- Central Africa: Finance cobalt or copper processing plants in DRC.
- Southern Africa: Co-invest in industrial real estate or logistics hubs in Johannesburg.
- East Africa: Fund large-scale renewable energy projects in Ethiopia or Kenya.

### Checklist: Due Diligence

1. **Regulations:** Are permits and licenses reliable?
2. **Currency:** How will exchange fluctuations impact returns?
3. **Infrastructure:** Are there hidden costs in transport, power, or logistics?
4. **Governance:** Does the company operate transparently?
5. **Community:** Is there local buy-in?

Skipping due diligence is the fastest path to failure.

### Diaspora Spotlight: A Framework in Action

A Sierra Leonean-American investor used the Three Horizons Model to shape her portfolio. She began with a retail shop (Horizon 1), reinvested profits into an agribusiness processing plant (Horizon 2), and committed to a healthcare training institute (Horizon 3). Each step built on the other, creating financial return and long-term social impact.

### Investor Insights

- Strategy transforms opportunity into wealth.
- Frameworks like Readiness and Three Horizons guide smart decisions.
- Regional strategies must be tailored, not generalized.
- Every investor — micro to major — benefits from structured planning.
- Diaspora networks thrive when they use models, not guesswork.

### Framework: Strategic Entry

1. **Assess Readiness:** Know your capital, risk tolerance, and goals.
2. **Choose Horizons:** Balance short, medium, and long-term projects.
3. **Adapt by Region:** Apply context-specific strategies.
4. **Scale with Partners:** Don't go alone — collaborate.
5. **Review Constantly:** Strategies must evolve with markets.

### Takeaway for Action

Vision without structure is wasted energy. Africa rewards investors who prepare, adapt regionally, and align short-term wins with long-term legacies. With the right frameworks, every level of investor can move from vision to action.

# CHAPTER SEVEN

## NAVIGATING REGULATIONS AND FINANCES: THE RULES

Every serious investor must grapple with risk. In Africa, the headlines often amplify risk while overlooking resilience. Both are real. Currency fluctuations, political uncertainty, and infrastructure gaps exist. But so does innovation, adaptation, and a track record of overcoming obstacles. Success belongs to those who can face risk directly — and build resilience into their strategy.

**Real vs. Perceived Risk**

- **Real Risks**: Currency volatility, inconsistent regulations, infrastructure challenges, political transitions.
- **Perceived Risks**: Outdated stereotypes of chaos, assumptions that all African countries share the same issues, or that corruption is the only way business gets done.

Distinguishing between the two separates cautious investors who retreat too early from bold investors who succeed long-term.

**How Resilience Works in Africa**

- **Entrepreneurial Spirit:** African entrepreneurs innovate around barriers (mobile money, solar mini-grids).

- **Community Support:** Businesses embedded in local communities survive shocks better than those disconnected.
- **Adaptation:** From drought-resistant crops to logistics tech, African ventures pivot quickly.

Resilience is not accidental. It is a strategy.

**Regional Spotlight: Risks and Resilience Across Africa**

**North Africa**

- Risks: Political transitions, heavy reliance on Europe for trade.
- Resilience: Strong tourism industry, renewable energy innovation (e.g., Morocco's solar projects).

**West Africa**

- Risks: Currency volatility, security in some zones.
- Resilience: Explosive fintech growth (Nigeria, Ghana) and cultural exports (music, film).

**East Africa**

- Risks: Regulatory hurdles and climate-related risks.
- Resilience: Strong innovation ecosystems (Kenya, Ethiopia), renewable energy, and regional trade.

**Central Africa**

- Risks: Governance instability and infrastructure gaps.

- Resilience: Vast natural resource base and growing regional integration efforts.

**Southern Africa**

- Risks: Energy crises and inequality.
- Resilience: Advanced financial markets, strong retail base, and industrial capacity.

**Investment Pathways: Managing Risk by Scale**

**Micro-Investment (under $10,000–$25,000)**

- West Africa: Join diaspora crowdfunding for fintech startups — high reward, regulatory risk.
- East Africa: Invest in small agribusiness cooperatives — climate risk, but food demand is strong.
- Southern Africa: Operate a small township transport service — operational risks, but consistent cash flow.

**Medium Investment ($25,000–$500,000)**

- North Africa: Boutique tourism in Egypt or Tunisia — political risk, but stable long-term demand.
- East Africa: Launch a mid-size dairy processing plant in Tanzania — infrastructure challenges, but strong consumer base.
- Central Africa: Regional logistics venture in Cameroon — governance risk, but limited competition.

**Major Investment ($500,000+)**

- Central Africa: Mining or energy processing in DRC — governance risk, but world-leading cobalt reserves.
- Southern Africa: Industrial real estate in Johannesburg — economic cycles, but hub status ensures demand.
- West Africa: Fintech expansion in Nigeria or Ghana — competition risk, but exponential scaling potential.

**Diaspora Spotlight: Resilience Through Persistence**

A Nigerian-American angel investor initially lost money in two early Lagos startups. Instead of withdrawing, he doubled down with better due diligence. Eventually, he backed a fintech firm that scaled across Africa and was acquired by a global tech giant. His resilience — the ability to learn from losses — transformed short-term setbacks into generational wealth.

**Investor Insights**

- Africa's risks are real but manageable.
- Resilience is often stronger in African markets than outsiders assume.
- Risks vary regionally; strategies must adapt to context.
- Every investment tier — micro to major — faces risks, but each also has resilience pathways.
- Diaspora investors succeed when persistence is paired with adaptability.

**Framework: Building Resilient Investments**

1. **Separate Real vs. Perceived Risk** — Focus on facts, not fear.
2. **Diversify Regionally & By Sector** — Spread exposure to minimize shocks.
3. **Embed in Communities** — Projects with community buy-in withstand crises.
4. **Use Risk Tools** — Political risk insurance, legal structures, and hedging.
5. **Adapt Continuously** — Be willing to pivot business models as conditions shift.

**Takeaway for Action**

Africa does not promise risk-free investment — but no fast-growing market does. Investors who prepare, diversify, and adapt discover that resilience is one of Africa's greatest assets. Risk is not the end of the story; it is the beginning of innovation, opportunity, and reward.

# CHAPTER EIGHT

## BUILDING A LEGACY: WEALTH WITH PURPOSE

The African diaspora is not separate from the continent's story — it is part of it. From forced migration through slavery to the voluntary migrations of today, Africans abroad have always influenced Africa's destiny. Today, the diaspora is more than a cultural bridge. It is a source of capital, networks, and vision that can transform Africa's economies.

**Historical Contributions**

- Diaspora intellectuals and activists supported independence struggles across Africa.
- Migrant remittances sustained families and communities for decades.
- Cultural influence — from reggae and jazz to hip hop and Afrobeats — kept Africa present in global consciousness.

The diaspora has always been a resource. What has changed is the **scale**: remittances exceed $50 billion annually, and structured diaspora investments are rising across every sector.

### The Diaspora Advantage

1. **Dual Perspective** — Familiarity with African culture and global financial systems.

2. **Access to Networks** — Capital, skills, and partnerships from abroad.

3. **Emotional Commitment** — A drive to link profit with purpose, wealth with legacy.

Where others see risk, diaspora investors often see home.

### Regional Spotlight: Diaspora Impact by Region

#### North Africa

- Diaspora communities in Europe invest heavily in real estate, tourism, and trade.

- Moroccan and Egyptian diaspora groups play key roles in manufacturing and logistics.

#### West Africa

- Nigerian, Ghanaian, and Senegalese diaspora communities lead fintech, entertainment, and agribusiness.

- Remittances here are among the highest in Africa, fueling education and small businesses.

**East Africa**

- Diaspora contributions fund startups in Kenya, Ethiopia, and Uganda.
- Somali diaspora networks have built powerful financial systems through hawala and community pooling.

**Central Africa**

- Congolese diaspora groups in Europe are investing in mining, logistics, and cultural industries.
- Partnerships with diaspora are often critical to overcoming governance challenges.

**Southern Africa**

- South Africans abroad increasingly invest in real estate, retail, and renewable energy back home.
- Diaspora in the U.S. and UK play roles in financing education and healthcare.

**Investment Pathways: Diaspora Capital at Every Level**

**Micro-Investment (under $10,000–$25,000)**

- West Africa: Diaspora savings groups funding cocoa cooperatives in Ghana.
- East Africa: Crowdfunding into fintech or agritech startups in Kenya.
- Southern Africa: Co-own small rental units or township businesses.

**Medium Investment ($25,000–$500,000)**

- North Africa: Diaspora-owned restaurants and eco-lodges in Morocco or Tunisia.
- East Africa: Mid-size dairy or horticulture ventures in Ethiopia and Tanzania.
- Central Africa: Logistics or small-scale manufacturing in Cameroon.

**Major Investment ($500,000+)**

- West Africa: Fintech firms scaling across Nigeria and Ghana.
- Central Africa: Energy and mining infrastructure in DRC.

- Southern Africa: Industrial real estate or renewable energy partnerships in South Africa.

**Diaspora Spotlights**

1. **Healthcare Builder:** A Ghanaian-British doctor invested in diagnostic centers in Accra, creating jobs and improving healthcare access.

2. **Tech Innovator:** A Nigerian-American software engineer co-founded a Lagos fintech, bridging Silicon Valley capital with African innovation.

3. **Agribusiness Entrepreneur:** A Kenyan-Canadian built a fresh produce export company linking local farmers with North American markets.

Each began at different scales of capital, but all shared vision, resilience, and a commitment to Africa's future.

**Investor Insights**

- The diaspora has always been central to Africa's economic story.

- Micro investments build communities; medium investments build businesses; major investments build industries.

- Regional diaspora patterns vary — but everywhere, they matter.
- Emotional commitment is a strength, but it must be paired with strategy.
- Diaspora investors succeed most when they combine local partnerships with global resources.

**Framework: Diaspora Investment Model**

1. **Start Small, Grow Steady** — Begin with micro investments or remittances structured as capital.
2. **Leverage Networks** — Diaspora associations, chambers, and alumni groups are powerful connectors.
3. **Choose the Right Scale** — Align with your financial ability, from micro to major.
4. **Stay Long-Term** — Commit to legacy, not quick returns.
5. **Build Bridges, Not Silos** — Work with locals as co-creators, not recipients.

### Takeaway for Action

The diaspora is not just a source of money. It is a source of vision, knowledge, and resilience. By channeling its resources into structured investments, the diaspora can build intergenerational wealth and shape Africa's transformation. The bridge between Africa and its global family has never been stronger. The time to cross it is now.

# CHAPTER NINE

## ACTION PLAN: STEPS TOWARD INVESTING IN AFRICA

Wealth without legacy is fragile. It can vanish in a generation, leaving no mark beyond the immediate moment. Legacy, by contrast, is wealth that endures — shaping families, communities, and nations for decades. For Africa and the diaspora, building legacy means more than preserving money. It means rewriting history, reclaiming agency, and ensuring future generations inherit strength, not struggle.

**Why Legacy Matters**

- Too often, businesses collapse when founders pass away.
- Land and property become contested without proper estate planning.
- Fortunes disappear when not reinvested into sustainable ventures.

Legacy matters because it:

- Transforms individual success into intergenerational wealth.
- Moves families and communities from survival to stability.

- Connects personal achievement with collective advancement.

### Financial Foundations of Legacy

Building legacy requires intentional planning:

- **Estate Planning:** Wills, trusts, and inheritance structures prevent disputes.
- **Business Succession:** Preparing the next generation to manage enterprises sustains value.
- **Diversification:** Balancing across sectors and geographies protects against shocks.
- **Education:** Passing financial knowledge to heirs ensures continuity.

These tools are not foreign. They are universal — and essential for wealth retention in Africa and the diaspora.

### Legacy Beyond Finance

Legacy also includes:

- **Culture:** Passing on language, traditions, and identity.
- **Community Impact:** Funding schools, clinics, and social enterprises.
- **Institutions:** Building organizations that last beyond individual lifetimes.

A true legacy is holistic.

### Regional Spotlight: Legacy in Action

**North Africa**

- Legacy is often tied to family-owned businesses and property.
- Example: Egyptian family enterprises in textiles or retail, passed down for generations.

**West Africa**

- Strong traditions of land ownership and community development.
- Example: Ghanaian entrepreneurs reinvesting in schools and community centers.

**East Africa**

- Family businesses in Kenya and Ethiopia often sustain agriculture and trade across generations.
- Legacy also includes education — diaspora families fund schools at home.

**Central Africa**

- Resource wealth has often been extracted, but diaspora investments are helping build lasting institutions.
- Example: Congolese diaspora supporting education initiatives in Kinshasa.

**Southern Africa**

- South Africa and Botswana showcase examples of business dynasties.

- Legacy is increasingly tied to institutional investment (pension funds, trusts).

**Investment Pathways: Legacy by Scale**

**Micro-Investment (under $10,000–$25,000)**

- West Africa: Purchase and retain farmland in Ghana or Nigeria for family inheritance.
- East Africa: Fund local school fees or micro-scholarship programs — building human capital as legacy.
- Southern Africa: Acquire and manage rental units for long-term family income.

**Medium Investment ($25,000–$500,000)**

- North Africa: Develop family-owned hospitality or retail businesses.
- East Africa: Build mid-size agro-processing businesses to pass on to heirs.
- Central Africa: Support small healthcare facilities that grow into community assets.

**Major Investment ($500,000+)**

- Southern Africa: Establish family foundations or endowments supporting education.
- West Africa: Finance manufacturing plants or financial institutions designed to last generations.

- Central Africa: Build large-scale infrastructure projects tied to family or diaspora legacies.

**Diaspora Spotlights**

1. **Senegalese Entrepreneur in France:** Began with remittances, then co-founded a mid-size agribusiness in Senegal. Today, his children manage the company, ensuring continuity.
2. **Jamaican-British Investor in Ghana:** Built healthcare clinics that outlast personal profit, preparing her children to expand them further.
3. **South African Diaspora in the U.S.:** Created a family foundation funding STEM scholarships in Cape Town, ensuring long-term impact beyond wealth.

**Investor Insights**

- Legacy is the difference between temporary wealth and generational power.
- It requires planning, diversification, and education.
- Regional traditions of inheritance and family business shape legacy strategies.
- Every scale of investment — from micro to major — can build legacy.
- Diaspora investors must think across borders, leaving impact in both home and host countries.

**Framework: Building Legacy Wealth**

1. **Plan Early:** Estate planning and succession must begin before crisis.
2. **Diversify:** Spread investments to preserve stability.
3. **Educate Heirs:** Pass down financial literacy and values, not just assets.
4. **Think Holistically:** Include culture and community in legacy planning.
5. **Build Institutions:** Foundations, businesses, and schools outlast individuals.

**Takeaway for Action**

Legacy is not just about money. It is about ensuring that the next generation inherits structures, knowledge, and values that allow them to flourish. For Africa and the diaspora, building legacy means converting today's opportunities into tomorrow's stability. Wealth may be temporary — but legacy, done right, lasts forever.

.

# CHAPTER TEN

## CASE STUDIES: REAL WORLD SUCCESS STORIES

While theories, strategies, and data are essential, nothing illustrates the African investment story better than real people and real journeys. These case studies showcase successes, lessons, and even failures from entrepreneurs and visionaries in various industries. They reflect the diversity of opportunities across the continent, the global Black diaspora's growing involvement, and the boldness required to take action.

These stories also highlight an important truth: Africa's opportunity is not a distant dream — it is already happening. Investors, creators, and entrepreneurs are building legacies on the continent today.

**Afrofuture (Ghana) — A Global Cultural Movement**

The founders of the AfroFuture festival (formerly Afrochella), Abdul Karim Abdullah and Kenny Agyapong Jr., launched the event in 2017 in Ghana to celebrate African culture and unite the global Black diaspora through music, food, art, and fashion. What began as a festival quickly grew into a cultural and economic movement, drawing thousands of tourists and generating millions in revenue for local businesses in Accra.

**Lesson:** Culture is one of Africa's greatest exports. When paired with tourism, it becomes a powerful driver of both economic growth and global connectivity.

**Steven Ndukwu (Nigeria) — Media as a Gateway to Investment**

Stephen Anthony Ndukwu, popularly known as Steven Ndukwu, is a Nigerian filmmaker, content curator, and media entrepreneur. His digital storytelling showcases Africa's lifestyle, real estate, and tourism opportunities to global audiences. By positioning himself as a trusted voice, Ndukwu has attracted both viewers and investors to projects across Nigeria and beyond.

**Lesson:** Media is not just entertainment — it is an entry point into markets, shaping perceptions and influencing where people choose to travel, live, and invest.

**Kea Wakesho Simmons (Kenya) — Travel and Relocation Through Traverze Culture**

Through her company **Traverze Culture**, Kea Wakesho Simmons empowers travelers to explore relocation, investment, and business opportunities through travel experiences. By blending cultural immersion with practical business exploration, Traverze Culture has become a bridge for diaspora members curious about moving to or investing in Africa.

**Lesson:** The future of travel is purposeful. Tourism is no longer just about sightseeing — it is also about scouting, investing, and creating a lifestyle connection to Africa.

**Mustapha Njie (Gambia) — Real Estate for the Masses**

Mustapha Njie, founder of **TAF Africa Global**, is one of the continent's most successful real estate developers. Known as "the Gambia mogul," Njie is on a mission to build one million affordable homes across sub-Saharan Africa by 2038. His projects in The Gambia, Nigeria, and beyond highlight how large-scale, affordable housing developments can transform both economies and communities.

**Lesson:** Real estate is not only about luxury. Affordable housing represents one of the most urgent and profitable investment frontiers in Africa.

**Dre Taylor (Ghana) — Beyond Investments and Diaspora Housing**

Dre Taylor, a real estate developer and social entrepreneur, is behind a major housing project in

Aburi, Ghana. His company, **Beyond Investments**, is building over 100 sustainable housing units designed with the diaspora in mind. Beyond Investments also supports dual citizenship initiatives, helping Africans in the diaspora reclaim their roots while investing in property.

**Lesson:** Real estate development tied to diaspora needs (housing, dual citizenship, community spaces) has enormous potential for both profit and social impact.

**Max Maxwell (Zanzibar, Tanzania) — Blu Pearl Luxury Villas**

Max Maxwell, an entrepreneur and investor, is building a $45 million luxury real estate project in Zanzibar: Blu Pearl Villas. The project includes 45 high-end villas on one of the most pristine beaches in the world. His journey highlights both the opportunities and challenges of luxury real estate in Africa — from navigating international regulations to managing large-scale construction in emerging markets.

**Lesson:** Big projects come with big risks — but also transformative rewards. Luxury real estate in Africa is increasingly attracting global investors who see the continent as a premier destination.

**Dr. Daniel (Nigeria) — Agribusiness at Scale**

Through **Farm Up Group**, Dr. Daniel has built two highly successful farms in Nigeria: a breeder farm generating $100,000 in monthly revenue and a commercial layer farm earning nearly $20,000 per month, both with profit margins above 40%. His work demonstrates how agriculture, one of Africa's oldest industries, remains one of its most profitable when done at scale with modern systems.

**Lesson:** Agriculture is not outdated — it is Africa's future. When paired with technology and efficiency, farming can generate returns that rival any other industry.

**Shofar Business Consultants (Namibia) — Diaspora-Focused Relocation and Investment**

Shofar Business Consultants offers curated tours and consulting services to help diaspora investors understand Namibia's business landscape. They provide relocation support, introductions to local business leaders, and strategies for establishing companies in Namibia.

**Lesson:** Consulting and concierge services reduce uncertainty. Having professionals who understand both diaspora needs and local realities makes entry into African markets smoother and more secure.

**John DeBellotte (Global) — Diaspora Freedom Initiative and Wealth Solutions**

John DeBellotte is the founder of Diaspora Freedom Initiative LLC, BIPOC Investment Group Ltd., and DeBellotte Global Limited. His companies specialize in comprehensive relocation, investment, and generational wealth solutions, providing expert support for entrepreneurs and families in the diaspora. By creating structured pathways and offering professional guidance, DeBellotte is reducing risk and opening the door for more people to confidently invest in Africa.

**Lesson:** Structured, professionalized support systems are critical. With the right guidance, the diaspora can move from hesitation to action, turning vision into sustainable legacy.

**Final Reflection**

These stories represent only a fraction of the movement underway. From culture to real estate, agribusiness to media, consulting to luxury projects — Africans on the continent and in the diaspora are reshaping the narrative of investment. Some projects are small-scale, others are massive; some focus on profit, others on purpose.

What unites them is a belief in Africa's potential and a willingness to act. As these case studies show, the window of opportunity is open — and those who seize it will not only benefit financially but also leave a legacy that spans generations.

# FINAL THOUGHT

Every generation faces a defining choice. For Africa and its global diaspora, the defining choice of our time is whether we will shape the continent's economic destiny or leave it to others. The past showed us what happens when Africa is defined by extraction. The present reveals a continent in transition. The future depends on the decisions we make today.

**From Potential to Reality**

Africa's story is often framed in terms of potential — its youthful population, rich resources, and cultural influence. But potential without action is wasted. The challenge is to turn potential into reality through investment, innovation, and collaboration.

**The Role of the Investor**

Investors are not bystanders; they are architects of the future. How capital is directed — toward extraction or value creation, toward short-term speculation or long-term legacy — will determine whether Africa's growth is inclusive and transformative.

The responsible investor asks:

- Does this create value locally?
- Does this empower communities?
- Does this build resilience?

**The Role of the Diaspora**

For the diaspora, investment is not only financial. It is cultural and historical. It is about repairing disconnections, building bridges, and reclaiming agency. The diaspora carries unique power: global capital, networks, and perspective. But its greatest strength is its bond — the will to see Africa prosper as part of family and identity.

**Regional Spotlight: Africa's Collective Path**

**North Africa**

- Next steps: Expand renewable energy, logistics, and tourism with stronger global ties.
- Path forward: Position as Africa's gateway to Europe and the Middle East.

**West Africa**

- Next steps: Harness fintech and cultural industries.

- Path forward: Translate creativity into scalable industries and value-added processing.

**East Africa**

- Next steps: Build on tech and agribusiness ecosystems.
- Path forward: Become a continental hub for innovation and renewable energy.

**Central Africa**

- Next steps: Manage governance while leveraging resource wealth.
- Path forward: Invest in value-added industries for minerals and energy.

**Southern Africa**

- Next steps: Revive energy systems, expand regional trade.
- Path forward: Use advanced markets to anchor Africa's industrial future.

**Investment Pathways: Entering the Future**

**Micro-Investment (under $10,000–$25,000)**

- West Africa: Fund a cultural content startup (film, music, digital).
- East Africa: Back a solar micro-grid in rural Kenya or Uganda.
- Southern Africa: Invest in small township retail or services with growth potential.

**Medium Investment ($25,000–$500,000)**

- North Africa: Develop boutique real estate or eco-tourism ventures.
- East Africa: Build agro-processing businesses tied to export markets.
- Central Africa: Launch logistics or service businesses bridging regional trade gaps.

**Major Investment ($500,000+)**

- West Africa: Support fintech firms scaling across Nigeria and Ghana.
- Central Africa: Finance mineral-processing hubs in DRC.
- Southern Africa: Co-invest in industrial and renewable infrastructure in South Africa.

**Diaspora Spotlights**

- **Bridge Builder:** A Somali-American network funds schools and small businesses in Somalia while building fintech links in Kenya.
- **Legacy Maker:** A Ghanaian family in the U.S. transitions from remittances to building commercial real estate in Accra.
- **Industry Shaper:** A Nigerian-British entrepreneur partners with global investors to expand West African fintech regionally.

These stories prove the diaspora is not just sending money — it is shaping the industries and legacies of tomorrow.

**Investor Insights**

- Africa's potential is real, but must be acted upon.
- Regional paths differ, but together they form a continental transformation.
- Micro, medium, and major investors each have a role in building the future.

- The diaspora is uniquely positioned to bridge global resources with African opportunity.
- The future belongs to those who start — no matter their scale.

**Framework: The Path Forward**

1. **Choose Your Role:** Micro, medium, or major investor — every level matters.
2. **Pick Your Region:** Align investment with regional strengths.
3. **Engage Partners:** Build locally, connect globally.
4. **Commit to Legacy:** Build wealth that outlives you.
5. **Act Now:** Waiting for the "perfect moment" means missing opportunity.

**Takeaway for Action**

The future of Africa is not predetermined. It will be shaped by those bold enough to invest — not just financially, but with vision and purpose. For the diaspora, this is not just opportunity. It is responsibility. It is legacy. The path forward is open. The question is: will we walk it?

# THE END

# APPENDIX

## Appendix: Regional Investment Cheat Sheets

### WEST AFRICA – REGIONAL OVERVIEW

West Africa is one of Africa's most dynamic subregions, with a population of over 420 million people across 15 countries. It is anchored by Nigeria, Africa's largest economy, and complemented by diverse markets such as Ghana, Côte d'Ivoire, and Senegal. The region is part of the Economic Community of West African States (ECOWAS), a 15-member bloc aiming for economic integration and, eventually, a single currency (the Eco).

Key regional characteristics:

- Population growth: West Africa's population is expected to double by 2050, making it a major consumer market.
- Urbanization: Cities such as Lagos, Accra, Abidjan, and Dakar are fast-growing hubs of finance, culture, and innovation.
- Sectors to watch: Fintech, agribusiness, real estate, creative industries, and renewable energy.
- Risks: Currency volatility (notably the Naira), political instability in some states, and infrastructure deficits.

- Opportunities: A large youthful workforce, cultural exports, digital adoption, and cross-border trade through ECOWAS.

**Country Deep Dives (Top 5)**

**Nigeria**

Population (2025 est.): 230 million
GDP Growth (2020–24 avg.): 3.1%
FDI Inflows (2023): $3.3 billion
Currency: Nigerian Naira (volatile, significant devaluations)
Urbanization: ~55%

Top Sectors

1. Technology & Fintech – Lagos is Africa's leading startup hub; fintech transactions exceed $200 billion annually.
2. Energy – Oil remains dominant, but renewables and gas-to-power projects are expanding.
3. Creative Industries – Nollywood, Afrobeats, and fashion are global exports.

Opportunities

- Mobile banking and digital services
- Agribusiness (rice, cassava, and poultry value chains)
- Diaspora-driven real estate in Lagos and Abuja

Risks

- Currency volatility and inflation

- Regulatory uncertainty
- Security challenges in certain regions

Investor Pathways

- Micro ($10k–25k): Back diaspora-led fintech startups via crowdfunding
- Medium ($25k–500k): Invest in agro-processing plants or digital media ventures
- Major ($500k+): Power infrastructure projects, industrial estates, or renewable energy ventures

**Ghana**

Population (2025 est.): 34.5 million
GDP Growth (2020–24 avg.): 4.3%
FDI Inflows (2023): $2.1 billion
Currency: Ghanaian Cedi (volatile; depreciation pressures)
Urbanization: ~58%

Top Sectors

1. Agribusiness – Cocoa, cashew, and horticulture processing
2. Renewable Energy – Solar and off-grid energy solutions
3. Real Estate – Diaspora demand for housing in Accra and Kumasi

Opportunities

- Value-add cocoa processing
- Renewable energy mini-grids for rural areas

- Tourism connected to the "Year of Return" initiative

Risks

- Currency instability
- Utility costs
- Bureaucratic hurdles

Investor Pathways

- Micro: Fund cooperatives for cocoa or cashew production
- Medium: Invest in agro-processing SMEs
- Major: Develop housing estates or renewable energy plants

**Senegal**

Population (2025 est.): 19.5 million
GDP Growth (2020–24 avg.): 5.0%
FDI Inflows (2023): $2.6 billion
Currency: West African CFA Franc (stable, pegged to euro)
Urbanization: ~48%

Top Sectors

1. Energy – Gas discoveries position Senegal as a future exporter
2. Agriculture – Fisheries and horticulture exports
3. Services – Dakar as a hub for finance and logistics

Opportunities

- Gas-to-power projects

- Agribusiness exports (mangoes, fish)
- ICT and services sector growth in Dakar

Risks

- Dependence on European markets
- Infrastructure gaps outside Dakar

Investor Pathways

- Micro: Diaspora co-ops in fisheries or horticulture
- Medium: Agribusiness processing for export
- Major: Gas projects, logistics, and industrial parks

**Côte d'Ivoire**

Population (2025 est.): 29.5 million
GDP Growth (2020–24 avg.): 6.1%
FDI Inflows (2023): $1.9 billion
Currency: West African CFA Franc
Urbanization: ~52%

Top Sectors

1. Agribusiness – World's top cocoa producer
2. Infrastructure – Major public works in Abidjan
3. Energy – Hydropower and gas investments

Opportunities

- Cocoa processing and export
- Industrial infrastructure in Abidjan
- Regional logistics through the Port of Abidjan

Risks

- Political tensions in election periods
- Export dependence

Investor Pathways

- Micro: Cooperatives in cocoa or cashew sectors
- Medium: Agro-processing for chocolate and cashew exports
- Major: Infrastructure and logistics projects in Abidjan

**Sierra Leone**

Population (2025 est.): 9.5 million
GDP Growth (2020–24 avg.): 4.5%
FDI Inflows (2023): $450 million
Currency: Sierra Leonean Leone (volatile)
Urbanization: ~43%

Top Sectors

1. Mining – Diamonds, rutile, and bauxite
2. Agriculture – Rice and palm oil
3. Tourism – Untapped coastal tourism potential

Opportunities

- Rice value chain development
- Eco-tourism ventures
- Mining services and equipment

Risks

- Currency instability
- Infrastructure and governance challenges

Investor Pathways

- Micro: Fund palm oil or rice farming co-ops
- Medium: Develop agro-processing and packaging SMEs
- Major: Industrial-scale mining or tourism infrastructure

**Directory Snapshots – Remaining West African Countries**

Benin – Population: 14.3 million. GDP Growth: 5.5%. Currency: CFA Franc. Sectors: Cotton, port logistics. Note: Emerging logistics hub with opportunities in agribusiness and trade.

Burkina Faso – Population: 23 million. GDP Growth: 3.2%. Currency: CFA Franc. Sectors: Gold mining, cotton. Note: Security challenges exist, but mining remains strong.

Cape Verde – Population: 600,000. GDP Growth: 4.0%. Currency: Cape Verdean Escudo. Sectors: Tourism, services. Note: Stable governance and strong tourism appeal.

Gambia – Population: 2.9 million. GDP Growth: 4.2%. Currency: Dalasi. Sectors: Tourism, agriculture. Note: Compact market with strong diaspora ties.

Guinea – Population: 14.5 million. GDP Growth: 5.1%. Currency: Guinean Franc. Sectors: Bauxite mining, energy. Note: World's top bauxite reserves; political risks present.

Guinea-Bissau – Population: 2.2 million. GDP Growth: 3.8%. Currency: CFA Franc. Sectors: Cashew nuts, fishing. Note: Small economy, niche opportunities in cashew exports.

Liberia – Population: 6 million. GDP Growth: 4.1%. Currency: Liberian Dollar. Sectors: Rubber, iron ore. Note: Post-conflict economy rebuilding; opportunities in agriculture.

Niger – Population: 28 million. GDP Growth: 5.0%. Currency: CFA Franc. Sectors: Uranium, agriculture. Note: Energy and agriculture potential but political risk is high.

Togo – Population: 9 million. GDP Growth: 4.7%. Currency: CFA Franc. Sectors: Logistics, phosphate. Note: Lomé Port makes Togo a regional trade hub.

**NORTH AFRICA – REGIONAL OVERVIEW**

North Africa is a strategically vital region linking Africa, Europe, and the Middle East. With over 210 million people and a strong tradition of trade, the region combines resource wealth with geographic advantage. It includes diverse economies such as Egypt, Morocco, and Algeria, which act as gateways for investment into the continent.

Key regional characteristics:

- Population: Over 210 million with high literacy and urbanization rates compared to other regions.
- Integration: Ties to the Arab Maghreb Union (though politically limited) and close trade relations with the EU.
- Sectors to watch: Energy (oil, gas, solar, wind), tourism, infrastructure, and manufacturing.

- Risks: Political instability in parts of the region, high youth unemployment, and regulatory complexity.
- Opportunities: Strategic trade corridors, renewable energy hubs, digital adoption, and established diaspora networks in Europe.

**Country Deep Dives (Top 5)**

**Egypt**

Population (2025 est.): 113 million
GDP Growth (2020–24 avg.): 3.9%
FDI Inflows (2023): $11 billion
Currency: Egyptian Pound (recent devaluations)
Urbanization: ~43%

Top Sectors

1. Energy – Oil, natural gas, and major solar projects.
2. Tourism – Ancient heritage and Red Sea resorts.
3. Manufacturing – Textiles, food processing, and automotive assembly.

Opportunities

- Renewable energy projects such as the Benban Solar Park.
- Real estate and infrastructure in Cairo and New Administrative Capital.
- Tourism expansion with post-COVID rebound.

Risks

- Currency volatility.

- Bureaucracy and regulatory challenges.
- Regional security concerns.

Investor Pathways

- Micro: Diaspora-led tourism and SME projects.
- Medium: Joint ventures in food processing or textiles.
- Major: Energy infrastructure, logistics, and large-scale manufacturing.

**Morocco**

Population (2025 est.): 38 million
GDP Growth (2020–24 avg.): 4.2%
FDI Inflows (2023): $3.7 billion
Currency: Moroccan Dirham (relatively stable)
Urbanization: ~64%

Top Sectors

1. Renewable Energy – Solar and wind investments.
2. Automotive – Manufacturing hub for Europe.
3. Tourism – Strong cultural and coastal appeal.

Opportunities

- North Africa's leader in renewable energy (Noor Ouarzazate solar complex).
- Automotive supply chain tied to European markets.
- High-end tourism and real estate.

Risks

- Dependence on European markets.
- Water scarcity in agriculture.

Investor Pathways

- Micro: Artisanal exports and eco-tourism ventures.
- Medium: Supply chain opportunities in automotive and textiles.
- Major: Renewable energy plants and industrial zones.

**Algeria**

Population (2025 est.): 46 million
GDP Growth (2020–24 avg.): 2.5%
FDI Inflows (2023): $1.2 billion
Currency: Algerian Dinar
Urbanization: ~73%

Top Sectors

1. Energy – Oil and natural gas dominate exports.
2. Infrastructure – Roads, ports, and housing development.
3. Agriculture – Cereals, fruits, and fisheries expansion.

Opportunities

- Energy projects with European demand for natural gas.
- Housing development in urban areas.
- Agriculture modernization and food processing.

Risks

- Heavy dependence on hydrocarbons.
- Bureaucracy and slow regulatory processes.
- Social and political tensions.

Investor Pathways

- Micro: Small agribusiness or fisheries projects.
- Medium: Food processing ventures.
- Major: Energy infrastructure and industrial housing projects.

**Tunisia**

Population (2025 est.): 13.5 million
GDP Growth (2020–24 avg.): 2.2%
FDI Inflows (2023): $700 million
Currency: Tunisian Dinar (moderately unstable)
Urbanization: ~70%

Top Sectors

1. Tourism – Mediterranean resorts.
2. Manufacturing – Electronics, textiles, and automotive components.
3. ICT – Growing digital services sector.

Opportunities

- Niche tourism, cultural heritage, and eco-tourism.
- Near-shoring for European supply chains in electronics and textiles.

- ICT outsourcing and startups.

Risks

- Political and fiscal instability.
- Youth unemployment.

Investor Pathways

- Micro: Diaspora investments in hospitality and tourism.
- Medium: Electronics and textile supply ventures.
- Major: ICT parks and large manufacturing facilities.

**Libya**

Population (2025 est.): 7.5 million
GDP Growth (2020–24 avg.): 2.0% (volatile due to conflict)
FDI Inflows (2023): Limited, <$500 million
Currency: Libyan Dinar
Urbanization: ~80%

Top Sectors

1. Oil and Gas – Among Africa's largest proven reserves.
2. Infrastructure – Massive rebuilding potential.
3. Services – Ports, finance, and logistics (long-term potential).

Opportunities

- Post-conflict reconstruction in housing, roads, and utilities.
- Oil sector rehabilitation and partnerships.

- Logistics and trade tied to Mediterranean location.

Risks

- Political instability and conflict risk.
- Weak institutional frameworks.

Investor Pathways

- Micro: Diaspora support in services or small trade.
- Medium: Construction partnerships during rebuilding.
- Major: Oil, gas, and infrastructure projects.

**Directory Snapshots – Remaining North African Countries**

Mauritania – Population: 5.3 million. GDP Growth: 4.7%. Currency: Ouguiya. Sectors: Mining (iron ore, gold), fisheries. Note: Growing mining potential and renewable energy projects; governance challenges persist.

Sudan – Population: 49 million. GDP Growth: 1.5%. Currency: Sudanese Pound (severe depreciation). Sectors: Agriculture (sorghum, sesame), gold mining. Note: Large agricultural potential, but political instability and conflict undermine investment security.

**EAST AFRICA – REGIONAL OVERVIEW**

East Africa is a fast-growing region with significant demographic and economic potential. Its population exceeds 290 million, and it is home to some of Africa's largest and most dynamic economies. The region combines agricultural abundance, rapidly expanding urban centers, and growing tech ecosystems, making it a hotspot for both domestic and international investment.

**Key regional characteristics:**

- Population: Over 290 million, with a youthful demographic and rising urbanization.
- Integration: East African Community (EAC) supports trade and economic integration.
- Sectors to watch: Agriculture, fintech, infrastructure, renewable energy, and tourism.
- Risks: Political instability, regulatory uncertainty, and infrastructure gaps.
- Opportunities: Digital finance, agricultural value chains, transport corridors, and industrial parks.

**Country Deep Dives (Top 5)**

**Kenya**

Population (2025 est.): 56 million
GDP Growth (2020–24 avg.): 5.0%
FDI Inflows (2023): $2.5 billion
Currency: Kenyan Shilling (moderately stable)
Urbanization: ~32%

**Top Sectors**

1. Agriculture – Coffee, tea, horticulture, and floriculture
2. Technology – Nairobi as a hub for fintech and startups
3. Infrastructure – Roads, ports (Mombasa), and energy projects

**Opportunities**

- Expansion of fintech and digital services
- Agricultural value-chain investments and agritech
- Transport and logistics linked to LAPSSET corridor

**Risks**

- Political volatility around elections
- Land ownership disputes
- Currency and inflation pressures

**Investor Pathways**

- Micro: Agribusiness, small fintech solutions
- Medium: Regional logistics, agritech, or tourism ventures
- Major: Infrastructure, energy, and industrial parks

**Ethiopia**

Population (2025 est.): 126 million
GDP Growth (2020–24 avg.): 6.5%
FDI Inflows (2023): $4.0 billion
Currency: Ethiopian Birr (managed float, periodic pressure)
Urbanization: ~22%

**Top Sectors**

1. Agriculture – Coffee, cereals, livestock, and horticulture
2. Manufacturing – Textiles, leather, and light industry
3. Infrastructure – Roads, rail, and energy (hydropower)

**Opportunities**

- Industrial parks under the "Made in Ethiopia" initiative
- Export-oriented manufacturing for African and global markets
- Hydropower projects and renewable energy

**Risks**

- Political instability and regional conflicts
- Currency restrictions and foreign exchange shortages

**Investor Pathways**

- Micro: Smallholder agribusiness ventures
- Medium: Manufacturing partnerships or agri-processing
- Major: Large-scale infrastructure and energy projects

**Tanzania**

Population (2025 est.): 67 million
GDP Growth (2020–24 avg.): 5.5%
FDI Inflows (2023): $2.0 billion
Currency: Tanzanian Shilling (stable)
Urbanization: ~37%

**Top Sectors**

1. Mining – Gold, gemstones, and industrial minerals
2. Agriculture – Coffee, tea, cashews, and sisal

3. Tourism – Wildlife parks and coastal resorts

**Opportunities**

- Mining development and partnerships
- Agribusiness modernization and export-oriented projects
- Eco-tourism and hospitality infrastructure

**Risks**

- Regulatory changes and resource nationalism
- Infrastructure gaps affecting logistics

**Investor Pathways**

- Micro: Local agribusiness or eco-tourism
- Medium: Mining partnerships and agro-processing
- Major: Industrial mining projects and tourism resorts

**Uganda**

Population (2025 est.): 49 million
GDP Growth (2020–24 avg.): 4.8%
FDI Inflows (2023): $1.2 billion
Currency: Ugandan Shilling (relatively stable)
Urbanization: ~25%

**Top Sectors**

1. Agriculture – Coffee, tea, and livestock
2. Energy – Hydropower and emerging oil sector
3. ICT – Mobile money and tech services

**Opportunities**

- Oil and gas exploration in Albertine region
- Renewable energy projects and hydropower expansion
- ICT startups and digital financial inclusion

**Risks**

- Infrastructure gaps and limited industrial base
- Political uncertainty and regulatory shifts

**Investor Pathways**

- Micro: Agritech, small-scale energy projects
- Medium: Oil services, ICT solutions, or agro-processing
- Major: Hydropower, oil infrastructure, and industrial parks

**Somalia**

Population (2025 est.): 19 million
GDP Growth (2020–24 avg.): 3.5%
FDI Inflows (2023): $300 million
Currency: Somali Shilling (volatile)
Urbanization: ~40%

**Top Sectors**

1. Livestock – Major export commodity
2. Ports and Logistics – Strategic access to Gulf of Aden

3. Telecommunications – Innovative mobile services despite instability

**Opportunities**

- Livestock export chains to Middle East markets
- Port development and logistics hubs
- Telecom expansion and fintech services

**Risks**

- Security concerns and political instability
- Weak institutional framework and rule of law

**Investor Pathways**

- Micro: Livestock farming and local trade
- Medium: Telecom partnerships or port logistics
- Major: Infrastructure and large-scale logistics projects

**Directory Snapshots – Remaining East African Countries**

Djibouti – Population: 1.1 million. GDP Growth: 5.0%. Currency: Djiboutian Franc. Sectors: Ports, logistics, and services. Note: Strategic trade hub, stable business climate, limited domestic market.

Eritrea – Population: 6.2 million. GDP Growth: 2.0%. Currency: Eritrean Nakfa. Sectors: Mining, fisheries, and agriculture. Note: Investment heavily restricted, high political risk.

Rwanda – Population: 14.5 million. GDP Growth: 5.8%. Currency: Rwandan Franc. Sectors: ICT, services, and agriculture. Note: Business-friendly policies, improving infrastructure, and growing tech ecosystem.

## SOUTHERN AFRICA – REGIONAL OVERVIEW

Southern Africa is rich in natural resources and strategically positioned for regional trade. Its population exceeds 70 million, and it includes resource-heavy economies like South Africa, Botswana, and Zambia. The region offers investment potential in mining, energy, agriculture, and tourism, though political and economic challenges vary across countries.

**Key regional characteristics:**

- Population: ~70 million, with moderate urbanization compared to other regions.
- Integration: Southern African Development Community (SADC) supports cross-border trade and policy coordination.
- Sectors to watch: Mining, energy, agriculture, tourism, and financial services.
- Risks: Political instability, commodity dependence, and infrastructure bottlenecks.
- Opportunities: Mineral exports, renewable energy, agribusiness, and high-end tourism.

### Country Deep Dives (Top 5)

### South Africa

Population (2025 est.): 60 million
GDP Growth (2020–24 avg.): 1.8%
FDI Inflows (2023): $5.0 billion

Currency: South African Rand (volatile)
Urbanization: ~67%

**Top Sectors**

1. Mining – Gold, platinum, coal, and diamonds
2. Financial Services – Banking, fintech, and insurance
3. Tourism – Wildlife and urban cultural hubs

**Opportunities**

- Mining and mineral beneficiation projects
- Renewable energy and solar/wind expansions
- Tourism and hospitality development

**Risks**

- Political and labor unrest
- Energy supply constraints
- Regulatory complexity

**Investor Pathways**

- Micro: Small-scale tourism or service ventures
- Medium: Financial services, renewable energy, or manufacturing partnerships
- Major: Mining infrastructure, industrial parks, and large-scale tourism

**Botswana**

Population (2025 est.): 2.7 million
GDP Growth (2020–24 avg.): 4.0%

FDI Inflows (2023): $1.0 billion
Currency: Pula (stable)
Urbanization: ~72%

**Top Sectors**

1. Diamonds – World-class production and export
2. Tourism – Wildlife safaris and luxury lodges
3. Agriculture – Cattle farming and small-scale crops

**Opportunities**

- Diamond beneficiation and jewelry manufacturing
- Eco-tourism and high-end safari lodges
- Agricultural modernization and value chains

**Risks**

- Economic dependence on diamonds
- Limited domestic market
- Climate variability affecting agriculture

**Investor Pathways**

- Micro: Small tourism or agribusiness
- Medium: Mining-related manufacturing or agritech
- Major: Luxury tourism, diamond beneficiation, or large-scale infrastructure

**Zambia**

Population (2025 est.): 20 million
GDP Growth (2020–24 avg.): 3.5%

FDI Inflows (2023): $1.5 billion
Currency: Zambian Kwacha (moderately volatile)
Urbanization: ~44%

**Top Sectors**

1. Mining – Copper, cobalt, and industrial minerals
2. Agriculture – Maize, tobacco, and horticulture
3. Energy – Hydropower potential

**Opportunities**

- Copper and cobalt projects for export
- Agro-processing and value-chain investments
- Hydropower and renewable energy development

**Risks**

- Currency and fiscal instability
- Dependence on commodity prices
- Infrastructure gaps

**Investor Pathways**

- Micro: Small agribusiness or trade ventures
- Medium: Mining services or agro-processing
- Major: Large-scale mining and energy projects

**Namibia**

Population (2025 est.): 2.6 million
GDP Growth (2020–24 avg.): 2.5%
FDI Inflows (2023): $800 million

Currency: Namibian Dollar (pegged to South African Rand)
Urbanization: ~49%

**Top Sectors**

1. Mining – Uranium, diamonds, and base metals
2. Fisheries – Marine resources and export
3. Tourism – Desert, wildlife, and coastal attractions

**Opportunities**

- Mining partnerships and beneficiation
- Fisheries development and export expansion
- High-end tourism and eco-lodges

**Risks**

- Small domestic market
- Dependence on commodity exports
- Vulnerability to climate change

**Investor Pathways**

- Micro: Fisheries and tourism ventures
- Medium: Mining supply chain or agribusiness
- Major: Industrial mining, fisheries processing, and luxury tourism

**Mozambique**

Population (2025 est.): 34 million
GDP Growth (2020–24 avg.): 4.0%
FDI Inflows (2023): $2.2 billion

Currency: Mozambican Metical (volatile)
Urbanization: ~39%

**Top Sectors**

1. Natural Gas – Offshore LNG projects
2. Agriculture – Cashew, sugar, and tropical fruits
3. Infrastructure – Ports, roads, and energy

**Opportunities**

- LNG development and export partnerships
- Agro-processing and commercial farming
- Infrastructure and logistics tied to ports

**Risks**

- Political instability in northern regions
- Security threats from insurgencies
- Currency volatility and regulatory hurdles

**Investor Pathways**

- Micro: Local agriculture or small trade
- Medium: Agro-processing, energy services, or logistics
- Major: LNG projects, infrastructure, and industrial parks

**Directory Snapshots – Remaining Southern African Countries**

Eswatini – Population: 1.2 million. GDP Growth: 3.0%. Currency: Lilangeni (pegged to ZAR). Sectors: Sugar, textiles, and tourism. Note: Stable but small economy with niche opportunities in agribusiness and tourism.

Lesotho – Population: 2.2 million. GDP Growth: 2.8%. Currency: Loti (pegged to ZAR). Sectors: Textiles, agriculture, and energy. Note: Limited industrial base, reliant on South African markets.

Malawi – Population: 21 million. GDP Growth: 3.5%. Currency: Kwacha. Sectors: Agriculture (tobacco, tea, maize), energy. Note: Agriculture-dominated economy, growing renewable energy potential.

Zimbabwe – Population: 16 million. GDP Growth: 2.0%. Currency: Multiple currencies in use. Sectors: Mining, agriculture, and tourism. Note: High potential but political and economic risks remain significant.

**CENTRAL AFRICA – REGIONAL OVERVIEW**

Central Africa is a resource-rich region with significant natural and human capital. With over 180 million people, it includes some of Africa's most mineral-rich countries and vast agricultural lands. The region is strategically important for energy, mining, and transport corridors but faces challenges in governance and infrastructure.

**Key regional characteristics:**

- Population: ~180 million, with high natural resource potential and growing urban centers.
- Integration: Economic Community of Central African States (ECCAS) supports trade and regional integration.

- Sectors to watch: Mining, energy, agriculture, infrastructure, and forestry.
- Risks: Political instability, corruption, and underdeveloped infrastructure.
- Opportunities: Mining partnerships, renewable energy projects, agribusiness, and logistics corridors.

**Country Deep Dives (Top 5)**

**Democratic Republic of Congo (DRC)**

Population (2025 est.): 107 million
GDP Growth (2020–24 avg.): 5.0%
FDI Inflows (2023): $3.0 billion
Currency: Congolese Franc (volatile)
Urbanization: ~45%

**Top Sectors**

1. Mining – Cobalt, copper, diamonds, and gold
2. Agriculture – Cassava, palm oil, coffee, and cocoa
3. Energy – Hydropower potential

**Opportunities**

- Mining partnerships and value-addition
- Agro-processing for domestic and regional markets
- Hydropower projects and energy infrastructure

**Risks**

- Political instability and conflict zones
- Weak regulatory and legal frameworks

- Infrastructure deficits

**Investor Pathways**

- Micro: Small agribusiness or artisanal mining
- Medium: Manufacturing and mining support services
- Major: Large-scale mining, hydropower, and industrial parks

**Cameroon**

Population (2025 est.): 29 million
GDP Growth (2020–24 avg.): 4.0%
FDI Inflows (2023): $1.5 billion
Currency: Central African CFA Franc (stable, pegged to Euro)
Urbanization: ~57%

**Top Sectors**

1. Agriculture – Cocoa, coffee, bananas, and rubber
2. Energy – Hydropower and oil
3. Manufacturing – Food processing and consumer goods

**Opportunities**

- Agro-processing and export-oriented agriculture
- Renewable energy projects
- Manufacturing and industrial zones

**Risks**

- Political tension in Anglophone regions

- Regulatory complexity and bureaucracy

**Investor Pathways**

- Micro: Small agribusiness or trade ventures
- Medium: Agro-processing, energy services
- Major: Industrial parks and hydropower projects

**Gabon**

Population (2025 est.): 2.4 million
GDP Growth (2020–24 avg.): 3.2%
FDI Inflows (2023): $600 million
Currency: Central African CFA Franc (stable)
Urbanization: ~90%

**Top Sectors**

1. Oil and Gas – Largest contributor to GDP
2. Mining – Manganese, gold, and iron ore
3. Forestry – Timber and sustainable logging

**Opportunities**

- Oil and gas partnerships
- Mining expansion and value-addition
- Eco-tourism and sustainable forestry

**Risks**

- Heavy dependence on oil revenues
- Small domestic market
- Limited diversification

**Investor Pathways**

- Micro: Forestry and local services
- Medium: Mining support services or agribusiness
- Major: Oil, gas, and mining infrastructure projects

**Republic of Congo (Congo-Brazzaville)**

Population (2025 est.): 6.3 million
GDP Growth (2020–24 avg.): 3.5%
FDI Inflows (2023): $400 million
Currency: Central African CFA Franc (stable)
Urbanization: ~70%

**Top Sectors**

1. Oil – Key export sector
2. Mining – Iron ore, potash, and gold
3. Timber – Logging and wood products

**Opportunities**

- Oil and gas investments
- Mining partnerships
- Sustainable forestry and value chains

**Risks**

- Political concentration and governance risks
- Infrastructure and logistics gaps

**Investor Pathways**

- Micro: Timber, local services, or trade

- Medium: Mining support and small oil services
- Major: Oil, mining, and industrial projects

**Chad**

Population (2025 est.): 18 million
GDP Growth (2020–24 avg.): 3.8%
FDI Inflows (2023): $250 million
Currency: Central African CFA Franc (stable)
Urbanization: ~23%

**Top Sectors**

1. Oil – Crude production for export
2. Agriculture – Sorghum, millet, and livestock
3. Mining – Gold and uranium potential

**Opportunities**

- Oil sector partnerships and infrastructure
- Agribusiness and value-chain development
- Mineral exploration and mining

**Risks**

- Political instability and security concerns
- Poor infrastructure and limited market access

**Investor Pathways**

- Micro: Small agribusiness or livestock ventures
- Medium: Mining services and agro-processing

- Major: Oil infrastructure, industrial parks, and mining projects

**Directory Snapshots – Remaining Central African Countries**

Central African Republic – Population: 5.8 million. GDP Growth: 2.5%. Currency: Central African CFA Franc. Sectors: Agriculture, timber, and gold. Note: High risk but untapped natural resources; security is a key concern.

Equatorial Guinea – Population: 1.6 million. GDP Growth: 3.0%. Currency: Central African CFA Franc. Sectors: Oil, gas, and timber. Note: Oil-dominated economy; political risk remains high.

São Tomé & Príncipe – Population: 0.2 million. GDP Growth: 2.5%. Currency: Dobra. Sectors: Tourism, cocoa, and fisheries. Note: Niche tourism opportunities; small domestic market.

**RECENT FDI SNAPSHOT**

**(AFRICA'S TOP DESTINATIONS, 2024)**

*Source: UNCTAD World Investment Report 2025, DabaFinance, World Bank*

| Country | FDI Inflows 2024 (USD, billions) | Growth vs 2023 | Main Sectors Attracting FDI | Notes |
|---|---|---|---|---|
| Egypt | 46.6 | +330% | Energy, real estate, infrastructure | Ras El-Hekma mega-project |

| Country | FDI Inflows 2024 (USD, billions) | Growth vs 2023 | Main Sectors Attracting FDI | Notes |
|---|---|---|---|---|
| | | | | boosted inflows |
| Ethiopia | 4.0 | +9% | Logistics, industrial parks, manufacturing | Remains East Africa's industrial hub |
| Côte d'Ivoire | 3.8 | +57% | Agribusiness, energy, logistics | Fastest-growing West African FDI market |
| Mozambique | 3.6 | +18% | LNG, mining, infrastructure | Gas projects dominate inflows |
| Uganda | 3.3 | +50% | Energy, oil pipeline, digital infrastructure | EAC growth hotspot |
| DR Congo | 3.1 | +12% | Mining (cobalt, copper), energy | Resource-rich, governance challenges |

| Country | FDI Inflows 2024 (USD, billions) | Growth vs 2023 | Main Sectors Attracting FDI | Notes |
|---|---|---|---|---|
| South Africa | 2.5 | -43% | Finance, mining, renewable energy | Decline due to investor caution |
| Namibia | 2.1 | -9% | Green hydrogen, renewable energy | Long-term energy play |
| Senegal | 2.0 | -56% | Energy, logistics, fisheries | Sharp drop due to project delays |
| Guinea | 1.8 | +64% | Mining, ports, logistics | Strong surge in extractives |

**Africa total inflows (2024): $97 billion** (+75% vs 2023). Africa now accounts for **6% of global FDI**, up from ~4% the year before.

**2. Country/Regional Risk Snapshot (2024)**

| Region / Countries | Political Stability | Currency & Inflation | Ease of Doing Business | Infrastructure | Overall Risk |
|---|---|---|---|---|---|
| North Africa (Egypt, Morocco, Tunisia) | [Med] | [Med] | [Low] | [Med] | Medium |
| West Africa (Nigeria, Ghana, Senegal, Côte d'Ivoire) | [High] | [High] | [Med] | [Med] | High–Medium |
| East Africa (Kenya, Ethiopia, Uganda, Rwanda) | [Med] | [Med] | [Low] | [Med] | Medium |
| Central Africa (DR Congo, Cameroon, Gabon) | [High] | [High] | [High] | [High] | High |

| Region / Countries | Political Stability | Currency & Inflation | Ease of Doing Business | Infrastructure | Overall Risk |
|---|---|---|---|---|---|
| Southern Africa (South Africa, Botswana, Namibia, Zambia) | [Med] | [Med] | [Med] | [Med] | Medium |

**Key takeaway:** Risk varies widely. Successful investors separate **real risks** from **perceived risks**, diversify by region, and engage trusted local partners.

## GENERAL INVESTMENT CHECKLIST

***Before You Invest in Africa – Key Steps***

### Mindset & Vision

- Am I approaching this as a **long-term builder** vs short-term speculator?
- Do I understand Africa's story through an **abundance lens**, not a scarcity one?

### Country & Sector Selection

- Which **region/country** aligns with my goals and capacity?
- Which **sector** (agriculture, energy, tech, real estate, culture, healthcare) matches my expertise or passion?

- Have I studied **diaspora case studies** and success stories in this sector?

**Risk & Due Diligence**

- Have I reviewed **political, currency, and regulatory risks** for my chosen country?
- Do I have a **diversification plan** across sectors or regions?
- Have I checked **permits, licenses, and tax obligations**?

**Partnerships & Networks**

- Do I have **trusted local partners** or advisors?
- Am I connected to **diaspora networks, chambers of commerce, or trade groups**?
- Have I engaged the **local community** where I plan to operate?

**Financial Readiness**

- What is my **entry level** (micro, medium, or major investment)?
- Do I have an **exit strategy** and a clear timeline (3, 7, or 10+ years)?
- Have I set aside a **buffer fund** for unexpected delays or shocks?

**Legacy & Impact**

- Am I building something that creates **value beyond profit** (jobs, skills, infrastructure, culture)?

- Do I have a **succession plan** for passing wealth to the next generation?

PAN AFRICAN LIFESTYLE

# AUTHORS BIO

Emmanuel Bope is a visionary entrepreneur, cultural strategist, and digital innovator whose work sits at the intersection of **Pan-Africanism**, entrepreneurship, and global connectivity. Born in the Democratic Republic of the Congo and raised in Canada, Emmanuel combines deep cultural heritage with professional expertise in branding, digital marketing, and business development.

As Co-Founder and CEO of **Pan African Lifestyle (PAL)**, Emmanuel has grown a bold idea — launched from a small basement in 2020 — into a global movement. Today, PAL reaches over half a million followers across multiple platforms, with digital content engaging between one and twenty-five million people from the Black diaspora each month. Under his leadership, PAL has published multiple works including *Africa 101: The Pan African Lifestyle Guide to Relocating, Investing &*

*Living the African Dream in the Motherland* and *Investing in Africa 101*, as well as innovative cultural projects such as the PAL Trivia and Umoja card games, a Pan-African music album featuring over 85 tracks, and apparel lines that celebrate African identity.

Emmanuel's expertise spans **branding, digital marketing, e-commerce, and strategic communications**. He holds diplomas in Public Relations, Marketing Communications, and a degree in Marketing Science, applying his knowledge to scale Pan-African entrepreneurship on a global level. His pioneering initiatives include **PANAFRICON**, the first major Pan-African conference, and the **PAL App**, designed to provide the diaspora with its own digital ecosystem for travel, relocation, investment, and community building.

As an author, speaker, and business leader, Emmanuel is recognized for advancing a modern vision of the African Dream — one rooted in collective empowerment, cultural pride, and sustainable economic growth.

**Solange Bope** is an entrepreneur, creative visionary, and brand strategist whose leadership blends African heritage with modern innovation in design, digital media, and cultural storytelling. Born in the Democratic Republic of the Congo and raised in Canada, Solange co-founded **Pan African Lifestyle (PAL)** in 2020 with the mission of making Pan-Africanism relevant and aspirational for a new generation.

As President of PAL, Solange has been instrumental in shaping its creative direction and digital expansion. From an idea many dismissed as impossible, she helped build PAL into a thriving community that now reaches millions globally through books, media, apparel, games, and music. She is co-author of *Africa 101: The Pan African Lifestyle Guide to Relocating, Investing & Living the African Dream in the Motherland* and *Investing in Africa 101*, publications that provide essential guidance for the global Black diaspora on relocation, investment, and building a Pan-African lifestyle.

Solange holds diplomas in Fashion Styling, Image Consulting, and Marketing Communications, which she integrates into PAL's diverse ventures. Her expertise lies in **branding, digital content strategy, and cultural entrepreneurship**, equipping communities to embrace Africa as both home and opportunity.

Together, Emmanuel and Solange lead **Pan African Lifestyle Inc.**, pioneering projects such as the PAL App and PANAFRICON to redefine what it means to live the African Dream. Their work has positioned them as authoritative voices in Pan-African entrepreneurship and digital culture — bridging tradition and innovation, and empowering the global Black diaspora to invest, create, and thrive.

www.ingramcontent.com/pod-product-compliance
Lightning Source LLC
Chambersburg PA
CBHW041300210926
51847CB00009B/83
*9781998780365*